T0352893

MAMMALS
OF KRUGER

Joan Young

Published by Struik Nature
(an imprint of Penguin Random House
South Africa (Pty) Ltd)
Reg. No. 1953/000441/07
The Estuaries No. 4, Oxbow Crescent,
Century Avenue, Century City, 7441
PO Box 1144, Cape Town, 8000
South Africa

Visit **www.penguinrandomhouse.co.za**
and join the Struik Nature Club for updates,
news, events and special offers.

First published in 2023

10 9 8 7 6 5 4 3 2 1

Publisher: Pippa Parker
Managing editor: Roelien Theron
Editor: Heléne Booyens
Cover designer: Janice Evans
Designer: Heléne Booyens
Picture researcher: Colette Stott
Proofreader: Emsie du Plessis

Reproduction by Studio Repro
Printed and bound in China by Toppan
Leefung Packaging and Printing
(Dongguan) Co., Ltd.

MIX
Paper from
responsible sources
FSC® C104723
www.fsc.org

ISBN 978 1 77584 819 6 (Print)
ISBN 978 1 77584 820 2 (ePub)

Contents

INTRODUCTION

The Kruger National Park is a world-famous game-viewing destination. Originally proclaimed by President Paul Kruger in 1889 and expanded in 1926, this natural wilderness now spans just under 20,000 square kilometres, an area larger than the country of Wales. Over 140 mammal species are found here, including the iconic Big Five: the elephant, lion, leopard, buffalo and black rhino.

This book will supplement your safari with interesting facts about the Park's diverse wildlife – from the fleet-footed cheetah to the secretive pangolin. Even the unassuming impala is capable of remarkable feats.

Successful safaris

Three factors determine game-spotting success:

WHEN: The best game-viewing times are in the early morning and late afternoon. During the heat of the day, most animals rest in the shade and are not easily spotted. It is best to set out as soon as the gates open in the morning, as many species spend the night on the warm tar roads. After 10am, when temperatures rise and most animals become inactive, find a nearby camp where you can have a bite to eat, a refreshing swim or a nap. Take another drive around 4pm. Guided night drives are a great opportunity to view nocturnal creatures.

WHERE: Different species live in different habitats. Some favour mountainous regions, others grassy plains. Some are always found close to permanent water, or in close association with termite mounds. Check the viewing notes under each species account as a starting point.

HOW: There is a knack to game viewing. Do not search for the whole outline of an animal – most of the time, grass and bushes will partially obscure it. Instead, search for movement and out-of-place patches of colour. Often a twitching tail or flicking ear will betray an animal's presence.

Note: Species that have not been sighted in many years, including the oribi and suni, have been omitted from this book, as have small, rare species, such as certain mongooses. Animals the average visitor will struggle to identify to species level – bats, rats and other small creatures – are treated in group accounts.

Game-viewing tips

- A good pair of binoculars is a must – never leave camp without them.
- Check the animal sightings board at your rest camp's reception. It will give you an idea of the recent movements of many species.
- Following the course of a river is generally rewarding, as most species will eventually visit to drink. There are also hippos, crocodiles and plenty of birdlife to see.
- Drive slowly and be patient. Many people race from place to place, but covering more ground does not mean you will see more.
- People tend to look far into the bush to spot game, but animals can often be seen lying quietly near the road.
- Birds can direct you to a sighting. Circling or landing vultures may suggest a kill, for example. Egrets rise from the feet of buffalo and blue wildebeest. These large creatures stir up insects as they walk, which the birds eat.
- Be on the lookout for dung. Big, fresh piles are a sign that large game such as elephants or buffaloes have recently passed. Do not drive over these piles – creatures such as dung beetles may be gathering material to build brood balls. Furthermore, elephant dung may contain thorns that can puncture a tyre.
- People in a stationary vehicle may alert you to something worth seeing. It is not considered impolite to ask them what they are looking at.
- Every now and then, switch off the car's engine and listen to the sounds of the bush. Often one then hears lions grunt, the alarm calls of birds and monkeys, or other sounds that indicate that something is nearby.

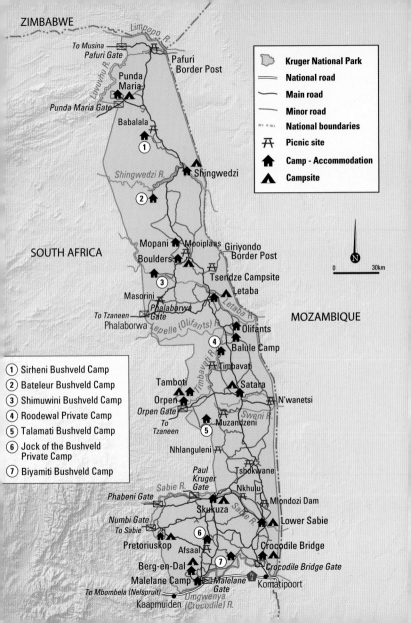

THE MAMMALS

Lion
King of beasts

Lions are the largest mammalian carnivores in Africa. As juveniles, males and females are difficult to tell apart. At around two years of age, the male's mane begins showing. It darkens with age, and may even turn black. A thick, dark mane indicates maturity and health – attractive to lionesses, and a warning to rivals.

Lions are the most social of cats, living in prides and often hunting as a group. Contrary to popular belief, a pride does not consist of a single alpha male, his females, and their young. Instead, a pride typically comprises two units: a core group of closely related adult females and their cubs, and an ever-changing coalition of males, who father the young and patrol the territory.

Whereas females stay in the pride they are born into, males are evicted at about three years of age. Brothers usually band together, and, when they are strong enough, will attempt to take over another pride by challenging the reigning males.

Lionesses have no mane, making them less conspicuous when creeping up on prey. As hunters, they are often more successful than big-maned males.

If the challengers manage to depose their rivals, males will kill all the cubs in their newly won pride. This ensures that their own bloodline is carried on, not that of the previous fathers. A lioness who has lost her young will come on heat shortly thereafter. She may mate with several males, copulating about every twenty minutes for two to three days.

Cubs are born blind, opening their eyes about a week after birth. Mothers often nurse one another's cubs and band together to defend the young from intruders, including new dominant males set on killing the cubs of a displaced male.

Lions roar to warn neighbouring rivals of their presence. They typically do so between dusk and dawn, when the sound carries furthest – often over five kilometres.

These predators are not man-eaters by nature. Typically, they only resort to this behaviour in desperation, after being kicked out of the pride owing to illness or old age.

Viewing notes: In summer, lions hunt at night and rest in the shade during the day. In winter, they can be active at any time. They often lounge on tar roads on cool mornings.

Lions are born with spots that fade with age.

Above: A male lion drives a female away from a carcass. She will feed after the males have had their fill. Cubs usually eat last. **Below:** A lioness swats at a suitor.

A family at rest. Note the young male whose mane is starting to show. He and his similarly aged male relatives will soon be evicted from the pride.

Leopard
Secretive and dangerous beauty

This handsomely spotted cat can be considered the Park's most dangerous large predator. Whereas a lion typically retreats when wounded, a hurt or cornered leopard will attack.

No two leopards have the same markings, and individuals can be recognised by the arrangement of rosettes and spots on their coat. In addition to prominent whiskers, very long hairs grow from a leopard's eyebrows. Sensitive facial hairs likely help this nocturnal hunter detect obstacles in its path as it makes its way through the bush.

Leopards are solitary and secretive. A male's home range may encompass those of several females, but he meets the occupants only to mate. The female gives birth in a sheltered den, such as a cave, and raises her litter alone. For the first few months, she conceals her young in a new lair every few days, lest they fall

The limbs are short but powerful.

prey to lions and hyaenas. Soon, they begin accompanying her to kills. While on the move, the white underside of the mother's tail tip provides a beacon for the young to follow. At about two years of age, the young leave to establish their own territory.

An opportunistic feeder, a leopard will consume anything from a mouse to an antelope twice its size. It is a master stalker, using every scrap of cover to creep up on its prey before pouncing. Impala make up an estimated 70% of its diet. Powerful muscles and strong, curved claws enable a leopard to drag a heavy carcass up a tree, where it can feed out of the reach of scavengers.

Unlike most lions, leopards are good swimmers and readily take to water.

Though quiet by nature, they sometimes vocalise with a harsh, rasping 'cough'. They also purr, and growl and grunt at threats.

Viewing notes: Elusive and nocturnal. Favours large trees near rivers, where it can rest, hunt and feed, and have easy access to water. In the early morning, it often scans its surroundings from high, rocky ledges or from a tree.

A mother grooms her cub.

Cheetah
Built for speed

The cheetah is the fastest mammal on the planet, with a small head, muscular shoulders, a thin waist, slender legs, and a long tail that acts as a rudder when changing direction at speed. Unlike other cats, its claws are only semi-retractable, affording it extra traction while running. The nostrils, lungs and heart are large to efficiently circulate oxygen and prevent overheating during a strenuous chase.

This cat feeds on medium-sized antelope such as impala, as well as smaller game, including hares, guineafowl and warthogs. When pursuing prey, a cheetah sprints at 80km/h on average, though some estimate its top speed to be 112km/h. It knocks its quarry off balance by hooking it with the large dewclaws on its front legs, and seizes the downed prey by the throat. Since its jaws are relatively weak and its teeth short, it strangles prey instead of delivering a killing bite like other cats. Many hunting attempts fail (as, incidentally, is true for all carnivores), and a successful kill usually leaves a cheetah panting and exhausted.

Left: It often perches on fallen trees, termite mounds or the Park's large stone route markers to scout for prey. **Above:** The cheetah has a streamlined build.

After catching its breath, it eats hastily, as it is no match for large scavengers such as lions and hyaenas that may steal its kill. By hunting during the day, it avoids competition with large nocturnal predators.

Though not as social as lions, cheetahs may be seen in small groups: often a female with her latest offspring, or two to five closely related males. Some males remain solitary.

Cheetahs do not roar. They purr when grooming or sitting near other cheetahs. When calling her young, a female will make a bird-like chirping sound. Cubs are born with a thick, pale mane that runs down their back. It has been theorised that their appearance mimics that of the fierce honey badger, making predators think twice before attacking.

Viewing notes: Favours open grasslands bordering the bush. The grasslands and more open terrain near Tshokwane and the H4-2 between Crocodile Bridge and Lower Sabie are good places to look out for cheetah.

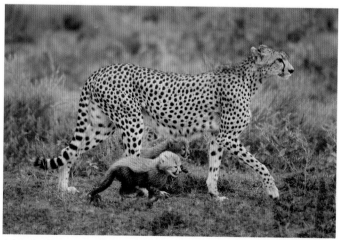

A female escorts her young. Note the cubs' dark body and pale, shaggy mane.

Siblings form coalitions once they leave their mother's care.

African wild dog
Boldly marked canine

This lean, long-legged canine has a strikingly patterned coat, large, round ears and a white-tipped tail. No two have the same markings, and the unique black, brown and off-white patterning can be used to distinguish between individuals.

African wild dogs live in packs. They have strong social bonds and there is a strict pecking order, with little infighting. A dominant male and female head the group. They are usually the only ones who breed, producing litters of two to seven pups (though litters as large as 20 have been recorded). Pups are born in underground dens, usually old aardvark burrows. All pack members assist in looking after the young. When a hunt ensues, some adult members stay behind to guard the youngsters. The denning period lasts only about 12 weeks, after which the pups accompany the pack.

There are strong bonds between members of a pack.

Wild dogs hunt during the day, typically early morning or late afternoon. They rely on sight rather than smell to find food. After picking their target, nothing will divert the pursuers from it, even if an alternative quarry passes nearby. They are not the speediest of hunters, but rely on their stamina to outlast prey, tiring out the animal until it can be pulled down, usually by a single dog. The rest quickly converge on the downed prey, rapidly tearing the carcass apart by disembowelling. They can strip a small antelope within 15 minutes. If there are pups nearby, they are given the opportunity to feed first. If not, the hunters eat their fill. They then head back to the den, where the pups and their caretakers beg for a meal by whining and licking the hunters' faces, prompting them to regurgitate chunks of meat. Pack members who are unable to hunt owing to illness or injury also receive a share.

Viewing notes: An estimated 300 African wild dogs are found in the Park. A well-known pack is often seen near Berg-en-Dal.

Adults tend to a large litter of pups. Like most dogs, their tails give an indication of their mood. An elder may put a paw on a youngster's neck to chastise unruly behaviour.

Spotted hyaena
Powerful, female-led predators

Of the three hyaena species in the Park, the spotted hyaena is the largest, measuring up to 90cm at the shoulder. It is solidly built, with a large head, muscular neck and sloped back. The irregular, dark spots that give it its name fade with age.

The spotted hyaena's reputation as a cowardly, slinking scavenger is undeserved. In truth, it is among Africa's most successful predators. Unlike big cats, it does not creep up on its prey. Instead, it boldly runs through a herd, and has an uncanny knack for spotting the weakest members before giving chase. It can reach speeds of 60km/h and maintain a pursuit over several kilometres. It possesses the strongest jaws of any mammal in Kruger, capable of crushing the thigh bone of a buffalo.

Hyaenas are all-rounders, scavenging as well as hunting. They work in tight-knit clans, and may even gang up on lions to steal a kill. They have an acute sense of smell and have been recorded detecting a carcass nearly two kilometres away.

Hyaenas and lions frequently clash over kills. Lions are larger, but hyaenas often outnumber their rivals.

Clans have a complex social structure and strict hierarchy, dominated by females. Even the highest-raking male is submissive to the lowest-ranking female. Females are larger than males and have very high levels of the male hormone testosterone. Females even possess a male-like sex organ, or 'pseudo-penis'. They urinate, copulate and, remarkably, give birth through this narrow canal.

Hyaena young are born in dens – anywhere from aardvark holes to culverts. Twins are the norm. Cubs are almost entirely black, and are born with open eyes and fully erupted canine teeth. At only a few minutes old, they squabble for dominance. Fights are especially fierce if both cubs are female, and the stronger cub may even kill its sister. Within the clan, daughters inherit their mother's rank.

Hyaenas are very vocal, and communicate with a range of whoops, cackles, giggles and whines.

Viewing notes: Most active at night, but often seen early in the morning. The highest densities are found in the central areas. They are often found around Crocodile Bridge and Lower Sabie.

Cubs are darkly coloured.

Brown hyaena
Rarely sighted scavenger

The brown hyaena is fairly large, with a dark, shaggy coat, striped legs, a cream or white collar, and a hairless black muzzle. It is primarily a scavenger, and its well-developed sense of smell can detect a kill nearly two kilometres away. Surviving on the carcasses of herbivores killed by other predators, it will steal portions as large as the ribcage. Its powerful forequarters enable it to carry heavy loads back to the den for its cubs. It also feeds on insects, reptiles, ground-living birds and their eggs, and wild fruits such as melons. Its ears grow up to 14cm long, and can pick up the faintest rustling of an insect in the grass.

Viewing notes: The brown hyaena is a vagrant species and is rarely sighted in the Park. It is typically nocturnal, but occasionally active in the early morning or late afternoon, especially in cool weather.

The forelegs are significantly longer and stouter than the hind legs.

Aardwolf
Termite hunter

This small member of the hyaena family weighs no more than 12kg. Its long-haired, yellowish-brown coat sports four or five vertical stripes. It is a specialised nocturnal forager, subsisting almost exclusively on termites. It uses its acute hearing to detect its insect prey, and laps up termites with a broad, sticky tongue. One aardwolf can consume up to 20,000 termites per night. Its sharp canine teeth can deliver a serious nip when fighting, but the rest of its teeth are reduced to small, peg-like stubs.

The aardwolf is an avid digger, altering old aardvark or springhare burrows to suit its sleeping and breeding needs.

Viewing notes: The aardwolf is associated with termite mounds. Over the winter months, when its favoured (nocturnal) termite prey becomes less active, the aardwolf will change its feeding habits and forage during the day, subsisting on diurnal termite species.

Aardwolfs are largely nocturnal.

Black-backed jackal
Versatile opportunist

The black-backed jackal is named for the broad, dark saddle of hair that covers the upper part of its back.

This opportunistic omnivore makes the most of what is available: scavenging for carrion, foraging for eggs, insects, fruit and berries, and preying on small antelope, rodents, birds, reptiles and amphibians.

Black-backed jackals mate for life. When their pups are young and still confined to the den, one parent heads out to find food while the other stays behind to tend to the young. Sometimes young of the previous year also help to feed the pups.

The wailing call of the jackal is a familiar part of the Park's evening chorus. A howling jackal is quickly answered by its family members, and then by other jackals in the area.

Viewing notes: More common in the Park's central savanna regions. Frequently seen on the eastern basalt plains. Several may gather around other predators' kills, waiting for a chance to dash in and grab a scrap.

Litters consist of up to six pups.

Side-striped jackal
Doting parent

The side-striped jackal is slightly larger and heavier than the black-backed jackal. It is characterised by a light-coloured, black-fringed lateral band on each flank, and a white-tipped tail.

As an omnivore, it lives on a variety of food items, from small mammals and carrion to wild fruit and insects and their larvae.

Strictly nocturnal, it shelters among piles of boulders or in disused aardvark burrows during the day. In the summer, when it is whelping time, burrows are altered to become more suitable breeding dens. Females with suckling pups will carry them, one-by-one, to a new den at the slightest hint of danger. Both parents help to rear the young after weaning and will regurgitate meals or carry scraps back to the den.

Viewing notes: Best seen on night drives. Especially found on the granitic soils in the west of the Park. Occasionally seen from the S1 along the Phabeni Road and around Olifants Camp in the early mornings or late afternoons.

The tail is bushy, with a white tip.

Bat-eared fox
A rare beauty

This small fox is instantly recognised by its enormous ears, which are up to 13cm long. When searching for prey – mostly termites, but also small reptiles, millipedes and spiders – it walks with its head low and ears pricked. It can detect the slightest underground sound, and rapidly digs up its meal.

Bat-eared foxes mate for life and forage in family groups. When the cubs are very young, the male guards their underground den while the female searches for food. These foxes are very social, frequently grooming each other.

They are fleet-footed, and escape predators by running at high speed and nimbly changing direction.

Viewing notes: A vagrant species, rarely sighted, but occasionally seen north of Letaba during dry years, where it frequents the mopane shrub. Active in the early morning and late afternoon. Lies up in holes or dense bush during the heat of the day.

Mother and cub.

Caracal
Handsome hunter

The caracal has striking facial features. Black stripes and white patches frame the eyes and mouth. The ears are tipped with prominent tufts of black hair, measuring some 4.5cm. The inner ear is covered with longish white hair. Individuals can be distinguished by the unique arrangement of their whiskers.

The caracal hunts a variety of prey, such as hares, hyraxes, young antelope, squirrels and mice, as well as reptiles. It leaps into the air to seize birds in flight. Like most cats, it is also a skilled climber.

As for most carnivores, it can go without water during time of drought and obtains enough fluid from its prey.

This nocturnal species is usually seen alone. If you are lucky, you may spot a female with her young.

Viewing notes: The S100 (Nwanetsi River Road) and the H14 (Mopani-Phalaborwa Road) are good for sightings while on night drives. Sometimes observed at the Duke waterhole south of Lower Sabie.

Above: The caracal is a short-tailed cat. **Right:** Kittens start eating meat at one to two months of age, and follow their mother to learn hunting skills.

43

Serval
A long-legged cat

This tall, slender cat has exceptionally long legs, and stands about 60cm at the shoulder. It hunts by sound, pricking the large, oval-shaped ears atop its small head to detect the rustling of prey in long grass. Once it pinpoints its target, this athletic predator will typically leap into the air or give a series of high bounds to pounce on its quarry. It moves between hunting areas on established game paths. Mice and rats make up most of the serval's diet, but it occasionally feeds on insects, lizards, frogs and scrub hares too. Using its strong hind legs, it is able to launch itself into the air to grab flying birds, including raptors – and can make a vertical leap of up to three metres. It will readily climb trees to raid bird nests.

This is a solitary species, but mating pairs will hunt together and mothers can be seen accompanied by their offspring. The female typically gives birth on a bed of leaf litter beneath a bush.

Viewing notes: Nocturnal and best seen on night drives. Occasionally spotted during the early mornings on the S32 close to Orpen, as well as at Transport Dam near Pretoriuskop.

Above: A serval leaps onto its prey. **Right:** A serval kitten

African wild cat
Ancestor of the house cat

This feline resembles a house cat, but is larger and has longer legs. Body colour ranges from grey to brown, with striped legs.

The African wild cat is the ancestor of all modern-day house cats. Some 10,000 years ago, members of this species were tamed and gradually domesticated.

Wild cats are solitary and fiercely territorial. Both sexes scent-mark their territories with urine and meet only to mate. Litters are born in burrows dug by other creatures, such as aardvark. Excellent climbers, these cats are often seen perched on tree branches. They hunt at night, catching mainly rats and mice but also birds, insects, frogs and solifugae (sun spiders).

Viewing notes: Best seen on night drives. May wander through chalets and camps.

The black-ringed tail is characteristic of this cat species.

African civet
Nightly visitor

The civet is grey, with a black facial mask and rows of dark spots along the body. When threatened, it erects a crest of dark dorsal hair, turns sideways for maximum effect, and may give a low growl.

It is active at night, and almost always found on the ground as it is a poor climber. Omnivorous, it moves down well-established paths with its head held low, looking for beetles, larvae, carrion, rodents, birds, eggs, small reptiles, frogs and fruit. The jaws are strong and muscular, but the teeth are blunt and not suited for chewing, so it holds larger prey in its paws while tearing bits off.

It marks its territory with a strong-smelling secretion from its anal glands. The smell takes up to three months to fade.

Viewing notes: Frequents camps at night. Found in forested areas and in high grass, typically near rivers and permanent watering holes.

Distinctive markings make the civet easy to identify.

Large-spotted genet
A sleek nocturnal predator

As its name implies, the large-spotted genet can be distinguished from its small-spotted relative by the sizeable, rusty-centred blotches along its body, as well as by its black-tipped tail.

During the day, it shelters in hollow logs, holes in trees, or old aardvark burrows. At night, it emerges to hunt rats, mice, locusts, beetles and birds. It feeds on wild fruits too. It will readily climb tree to escape danger or raid birds' nests, and has been known to leap from tree to tree, clearing distances of 3–4m.

It is solitary by nature, but occasionally a breeding pair will be seen together. Under stress, this genet will emit a musky odour from its anal gland.

Viewing notes: Present throughout the Park, and more abundant than the small-spotted genet.

Small-spotted genet
A lookalike with a white-tipped tail

This species is distinguished by its small spots, which lack a rusty centre, and white-tipped tail. It is a proficient and fleet-footed hunter, moving with its body kept low and tail held horizontally. It will also scramble up trees in the search for food.

It mainly preys on reptiles, millipedes, insects and spiders, but its varied diet may include rodents, guineafowl and other birds, frogs and small mammals such as rabbits. It grabs its prey in sharp claws, then bites it into pieces and swallows without much chewing.

Nocturnal, it shelters in hollow logs, holes in trees, dense bush or piles of boulders during the day. Females typically bear their young in underground burrows. They utilise disused aardvark or hare burrows, as their claws are not suited to digging.

Viewing notes: More common in the southern regions.

Note the white-tipped tail.

Honey badger
Formidable fighter

Despite weighing no more than 12kg, this small mammal has a reputation for ferocity. Other animals tend to give it a wide berth, as a honey badger thinks little of attacking predators much larger than itself, such as leopards and lions. Its skin is exceptionally tough – impenetrable to bee stings, porcupine quills and even snake fangs – and loosely attached. Should a predator seize it by the neck, a badger can literally turn inside its skin to reach the attacker. It also emits a foul-smelling odour from its anal glands when provoked.

A badger will eat just about anything, including rodents, insects, spiders, scorpions, lizards, snakes, carrion and fruit. It forages at a slow, winding pace, padding quietly on thick-soled paws, and constantly sniffing for food. It is known to scramble up trees to raid bee hives. Its claws are large and extremely sharp, used to dig for termites, eggs and grubs, and its powerful jaws can crush tortoise shells.

Viewing notes: Mainly nocturnal, but may hunt during the day in cool weather or during the winter, when food is scarce. Occasionally seen on night drives near Satara Camp, Talamati Bushveld Camp and the S29.

A small but ferocious predator.

Cape clawless otter
Sleek swimmer

This aquatic mammal has a smooth, dense coat with dark brown upperparts and lighter underparts. Its tail is short, flattened and used to propel it through water. Its feet are partly webbed and clawless, and well suited to digging through mud and searching for prey, such as crabs, fish and snails. It grabs its meal with its forepaws, uses its strong teeth to chew it, and then swallows it shell fragments and all.

While foraging underwater, it is able to seal its nostrils shut. Equipped with formidable canine teeth, it can inflict serious bites if attacked.

Viewing notes: Rarely seen. Frequents dams, lakes or streams, especially in the early mornings or late afternoons. Typically swims close to the surface. In the heat of the day, it rests in dry and sheltered places, reed beds or in holes in the ground.

The flat tail is used to propel it forward when swimming.

Striped polecat (zorilla)
The 'African skunk'

The striped polecat is easily recognised by its bold black-and-white markings and long, silky coat. If disturbed or cornered, it puts on a fearsome display. It raises the hair on its back, appearing to double in size, lifts its tail, and screams loudly. Turning its rear end towards the harasser, it ejects a pungent anal fluid. This nauseating, long-lasting stink is the origin of the expression 'to smell like a polecat'.

Ground-living, the polecat shelters in disused holes, rock crevasses or under fallen trees, and will dig its own burrow if necessary. It may climb trees to escape persistent predators.

It births litters of one to three young, which are hairless but already sport black stripes on their pink bodies.

Viewing notes: Uncommon and seldom seen. Active at night, favouring grasslands, rocky areas, thorny bush and savannas.

The striped polecat is rarely spotted, but unmistakeable.

Banded mongoose
Highly sociable

This mongoose is easily identified by the series of black bands on its long-haired, greyish-brown coat. It lives in packs of about 20 individuals, though groups as large as 75 have been recorded.

While foraging, the pack scatters and keeps in touch through high-pitched twittering. Its diet is varied, and includes grubs, millipedes, frogs and small reptiles. If a mongoose comes across a bird's egg, it will pick it up with its forepaws and hurl it through its back legs onto a rock until it breaks, then it will eat the yolk.

They typically clamber onto termite mounds to keep watch for predators, such as eagles and wild dogs. When a potential threat is detected, they stop in their tracks, stand up on their hind legs, and scan their surroundings. If the danger is real, the pack will flee down nearby holes, into hollow logs or dug-out termite mounds.

Viewing notes: Seen only during daylight hours. Frequently observed dashing across roads.

The parallel black bands help distinguish this mongoose from others in the Park.

Dwarf mongoose
The smallest mongoose

The dwarf mongoose measures just 40cm in length, half of which is its tail. It lives in groups of eight to ten members. Mutual grooming is a favourite pastime, and it spends many hours in this way. Only the dominant female breeds, giving birth to litters of up to seven pups. She typically has two litters in summer, when insects are plentiful. Some females have been recorded to birth five litters in a single breeding season. Younger members help to raise the young, since the mother must forage and feed well to sustain herself and produce enough milk for her offspring.

Dwarf mongooses use old termite mounds as dens, digging multiple entrances and tunnels with their strong claws. They are not dependent on water, as they get enough moisture from the food they eat. When they do drink from a watering hole, they dip their paws into the water and lick the moisture off them.

Viewing notes: Best seen around old termite mounds. Active during daylight hours, but stays inside on cold or rainy days.

The dwarf mongoose is uniformly brown.

Dwarf mongooses shelter in old termite mounds.

Slender mongoose
A distinctive tail

This short-legged mongoose is characterised by a long, thin tail tipped with black hair. The colour of its coat varies considerably, from reddish brown to grey. While running, the body is kept close to the ground and the tail is held out straight, with the tip curled up.

If excited or on the defence, the slender mongoose will erect the hairs on its body and tail so as to appear bigger. It typically shelters in holes in the ground, but may use rocks, fallen trees or tree hollows. It often climbs trees to escape danger.

It is solitary and active during the day, but does not emerge if the weather is too overcast or cold. It feeds on insects, especially grasshoppers, but will also eat mice, wild fruit and lizards. One or two young are born in the summer, when food is readily available.

Viewing notes: Mainly seen when dashing across roads bordering open grasslands. Rapidly disappears into the grass if approached.

Note the upturned tail tip.

Yellow mongoose
Solitary forager

This small mongoose varies in colour, from tawny yellow to grizzled grey. The coat becomes long and shaggy during winter.

It lives in colonies of eight to ten individuals. It has strong claws and is an skilled digger, but may occupy ready-made burrows dug by other animals.

Despite inhabiting communal warrens, the group usually splits up at daybreak, moving along established paths and foraging alone. They feed mainly on beetle larvae, ants and termites, but may eat grasshoppers, crickets and occasionally small birds.

Viewing notes: Active during the day.

The tail is quite bushy, usually with a white tip.

Selous's mongoose

Meller's mongoose

Other mongooses
Seldom seen or poorly known

Selous's mongoose is tawny brown or greyish. It is solitary and nocturnal. When hunting, it walks with its head held low, stopping now and then to sit up on its back legs, looking and listening for possible danger. It eats almost any small thing that crosses its path, including insects, mice, frogs, small birds and lizards.

Meller's mongoose is large, measuring up to 80cm from nose to tail. It has thick, coarse brown hair. It is solitary and nocturnal, feeding mainly on harvester termites. When food is scarce, it will also eat grasshoppers, small reptiles, millipedes, beetles and frogs.

The **white-tailed mongoose** has a brown-grey, shaggy coat and bushy, mainly white tail. Insects are its favoured prey, but it will also eat fruit, rodents, frogs and reptiles. It is nocturnal and typically solitary, but is occasionally seen in small family parties.

White-tailed mongoose

African elephant
Giant of the bushveld

Elephants are the largest land animals on Earth, with some mature bulls weighing 6,000kg and measuring four metres at the shoulder. Both sexes have tusks, a set of ever-growing incisors used as weapons and to strip the bark from trees, snap branches, lift objects and dig for roots.

The boneless, highly sensitive trunk is controlled by over 50,000 muscles (the entire human body, in contrast, has only about 600). It is nimble enough to pluck a single flower, and strong enough to uproot a tree. The trunk is used to feed, to breathe and smell, to communicate and even to snorkel in deep water. An elephant drinks by sucking water into its trunk, then squirting it into its mouth. A fully grown adult can consume up to 160 litres of water and 300kg of vegetation a day. It has six sets of molars during its lifetime. When the final set is worn down, the elephant is incapable of chewing properly, and will likely starve to death. The typical lifespan is 50 years.

An adult elephant is caught napping as it supports itself against a tree.

Despite its size, an elephant moves stealthily. The sole of the foot is thick and elastic, cushioning its steps. The cracks on the sole are as unique as fingerprint, and can be used to identify individuals.

Highly social, elephants live in herds consisting of a matriarch (an older cow who leads the herd), her female descendants, and their young. Male offspring are forced to leave the herd and form bachelor groups. When old enough, they will briefly join a female herd to mate. Every year, an adult bull enters a period known as 'musth'. Its testosterone levels rise significantly, it becomes aggressive towards other males, and it covers great distances in search of females. A bull in musth can be distinguished by the dark, oily substance secreted from the gland situated between its eye and ear.

Cows have the longest gestation of any mammal – up to 22 months. Newborns weigh about 120kg.

Viewing notes: Elephants cover vast areas in search of food, but are never far from water. The best chance of seeing them on a short visit is to follow the main road from Skukuza to Lower Sabie.

Left: A fine network of shallow blood vessels runs through the back of an elephant's ear. Flapping the ears cools the blood, preventing the animal from overheating. Elephants do not sweat. **Right:** The trunk is highly mobile.

The herd's matriarch leads them to grazing and water. When disturbed, the herd looks to her. If she charges – or takes flight – they follow her example.

Buffalo
Unpredictable bovine

This massive, bulky grazer weighs about 800kg when fully mature. Both sexes have heavy, hooked horns, although only the male has a 'boss' – a thick, helmet-like shield on top of its head, where its horns meet. The horn tips of an adult bull can measure up to a metre apart.

Despite its bulk, a buffalo can attain a speed of up to 45km/h when charging. It is famed for its ferocity, and is dangerous and unpredictable. If one buffalo is under attack, the rest of the herd will rush to its defence. A herd is capable of driving an entire pride of lions off.

This species is short-sighted, and will stare intently in the direction of the slightest sound.

Viewing notes: Always found near water. If you spend some time at Nyamundwa Dam near Phabeni Gate or Nhlanganini Dam near Letaba, you are bound to see them.

Like all antelope, the buffalo does not have front teeth (incisors and canines) in its upper jaw. It feeds by shredding grass between its bottom teeth and the hard 'dental pad' in its upper jaw.

Buffalo wallow to keep cool during the heat of the day. They live in large herds, usually about 100 animals. Congregations of 1,000 or more may be encountered, but will usually break up in the dry season, when resources are scarce.

White rhinoceros
The second-largest land animal

White rhino bulls stand 1.8m at the shoulder, and weigh up to 2,000kg, making them second only the elephant in size. Both male and female rhinos sport a pair of horns, the front horn being larger and longer. Horns are not made of bone, nor are they attached to the skull itself. They grow on the rhino's skin, and are composed of keratin – the same substance that fingernails and hair are made of. Horns are used as a defensive weapon, to dig for water, and to break branches.

The white rhino is named for its wide lips, not the colour of its body (which is grey). The broad, square muzzle earned it the moniker 'wide' rhino (or 'wyd' in Afrikaans), which became 'white' rhino over time. These wide lips are well suited to cropping short grasses.

White rhino mothers usher their calves along in front of them. In contrast, black rhino calves walk behind their mothers.

This species is dependent on water, and drinks regularly. In summer, it often lies in pools to keep cool. It frequently indulges in mud-wallowing. When the mud on its body has dried, it rubs against trunks or boulders to dislodge mud-encased ticks. Favourite rubbing trees become debarked and polished over time.

The white rhino is short-sighted, and has trouble detecting a motionless creature at 30m. Its hearing and sense of smell are well developed, however.

A dominant white rhino bull has a clearly defined domain, and marks the borders by scattering its dung with its hind feet and spraying urine onto bushes. Submissive males are allowed within this territory, but challengers are met with charges and horn clashes. The white rhino is more social than the solitary black rhino, and is often found in small family parties.

Viewing notes: Signs of rhino dung are sure indicators of their presence nearby. Look for dung in the area around Berg-en-Dal, Pretoriuskop, and towards Skukuza. Rhinos can become very accustomed to the cars and are sometimes seen lying on the warm tar roads in the early morning.

A white rhino scatters its dung.

Above: The white rhino can also be distinguished from the black rhino by the hump in the middle of its back. **Below:** It is fond of bathing in mud.

Black rhinoceros
The 'Big Five' rhino

The black rhino resembles the white rhino, but is slightly smaller, with a hooked lip instead of a broad mouth. Unlike its grazing relative, the black rhino is a browser, using its mobile upper lip to grasp twigs and shoots from shrubs and trees.

It is one of the Big Five, a title originally bestowed on animals considered the most dangerous to hunt. A provoked black rhino is more aggressive than a white rhino, and very agile. Even at a gallop, it can practically turn on a dime.

The black rhino is quite vocal. The female emits high-pitched mews to call her calf. When males fight for the right to mate, they vocalise with snorts, squeals and screams (the white rhino, by contrast, skirmishes in silence).

This rhino is solitary, but not territorial, making use of communal dung heaps known as middens.

Viewing notes: Rarer than the white rhino. Sometimes seen along the Sweni and N'waswitsontso rivers. Favours thick bush in which to shelter.

Oxpeckers pick ticks from a black rhino's skin, ridding it of parasites.

Hippopotamus
Semi-amphibious giant

This massive herbivore spends its days in water and grazes on land during the night. Its small nostrils, eyes and ears are situated along the top of its head, poking out of the water when the rest of the body is submerged. It can hold its breath for up to six minutes.

A hippo may look sluggish, but it is Africa's deadliest mammal. Armed with formidable teeth, it is quick to attack perceived threats, such as humans finding themselves on its path to the water. Despite weighing over 1,500kg, an adult hippo can charge at 30km/h – or just over eight metres a second.

Hippo skin is almost five centimetres thick, a record among land mammals. It exudes a reddish fluid when exposed to harsh sunlight. This ooze functions as a type of antibacterial sunscreen.

Viewing notes: A sure sighting at almost any of the Park's rivers and dams. The best time to see hippos out of the water is during the winter or on cloudy days, when they emerge to sunbathe on the banks.

Its jaws can open almost 180 degrees, and the tusk-like canines can reach a length of 50cm.

Hippos comfortably live alongside crocodiles. Predators are wary of targeting even a small hippo calf. A female hippo bears only one young about every three years, and is fierce in its defence.

Giraffe
Tall and inquisitive

An adult giraffe is around five metres tall, two metres of which is its remarkably long neck. Like humans and most other mammals, giraffes have only seven vertebrae in their neck – but these bones are greatly lengthened. The patchwork coat pattern is unique to each giraffe, and darkens with age. Both sexes have knob-like, skin-covered 'horns', known as ossicones. They are topped with tufts of hair in the female, and thicker, with bald tops, in the male.

Circulating blood through such a large, elongated body comes with unique challenges. To prevent the giraffe from getting dizzy when it lowers or raises its head, an intricate system of valves regulates the flow of blood to the brain.

Giraffes are inquisitive and quick to notice oddities. If one member of the herd spots something out of place, the rest will join it in staring, and even move closer to get a better view.

Though it appears to run in slow-motion, the giraffe's strange, loping run covers considerable ground. In fact, when fleeing predators, it can attain a speed of over 50km/h. Its strong hooves and powerful kicks are its greatest defence.

Above: Giraffes are very cautious around waterholes, as bending down to drink leaves them vulnerable. **Right:** They have brown eyes and long eyelashes.

Every day, a giraffe will spend 15–20 hours feeding, using its great height to browse leaves that are out of other animals' reach. A prehensile tongue, 40–50cm in length, enables it to deftly grasp and pull fresh shoots into its mouth, even among tangles of thorns. The leaves and flowers of acacia thorn trees are a favourite meal. Giraffe lips are thick and leathery, offering further protection against thorns and prickles.

Giraffes are known to chew old bones to supplement the calcium deficiencies in their diet.

Gestation is longer than a year – 15 months – and a single calf weighing 100kg is born. Mothers give birth standing up, and the newborn drops about 1.5m to the ground. It is able to get to its feet and walk within an hour.

Viewing notes: More than two-thirds of South Africa's giraffes occur in the Park. The highest densities occur in the Satara and Crocodile Bridge areas. They are mostly seen among impala, zebra and blue wildebeest, as the combined watchfulness of several species benefits all of them.

Above: The purplish-black coloration of the long, prehensile tongue may protect it from getting sunburnt. **Right:** To rid their belly of ticks, they may rub themselves on low bushes.

Bulls fight for the right to mate with cows by hitting each other with sweeping blows of the neck and head. Fights are usually resolved when one bull is too exhausted to continue. Courting giraffes 'neck' each other gently.

Burchell's zebra
Iconic equine

No two zebras have the same stripe pattern, and an individual's left and right sides are not symmetrical. The purpose of these bold stripes is still the subject of much discussion. It is possible that they deter biting insects.

Like horses, zebras live in herds made up of many families. A dominant stallion guards its mares and offspring from rival males and other intruders. Young males form bachelor groups until they are mature enough to start their own harem by stealing fillies of breeding age.

A zebra's hooves and teeth make a formidable defence, so pulling down an adult zebra is a difficult task.

In the heat of the day, zebras angle themselves to face the sun so that it falls on as little of the body as possible. They have been known to dig for water when necessary.

Viewing notes: These grazers favour scrub country and grasslands close to water. They prefer grazing on coarse, fibrous grasses, and are often found alongside antelope that eat finer grasses.

Above: Zebra foal. **Right:** A herd grazing among impala.

93

Ears pricked, these zebras are alert to danger as they drink.

Warthog
An odd-looking but endearing pig

With its lumpy face, large tusks, and antenna-like tail, the warthog is unmistakeable. The 'warts' that give it its name are in truth thick growths of skin. Males have four, and females two. Both sexes have two pairs of tusks. The smaller, lower pair is very sharp, and can injure predators as large as leopards. A warthog under threat often takes up a defensive position by reversing into a disused burrow, presenting the attacker with its formidable tusks.

The warthog mainly grazes, usually while kneeling on its calloused wrists, and also unearths roots and bulbs with its tusks and snout. Strictly speaking, it is an omnivore, as it may feed opportunistically on earthworms, insects and eggs.

Warthog families stick together when on the move, often running in a line with their tails erect.

Viewing notes: Commonly seen in grasslands, often in the company of mixed herds of impala, zebra, blue wildebeest and giraffe.

A pair of warthogs 'kneel' while feeding. They live in groups known as sounders.

Bushpig
Nocturnal hog

Bushpigs resemble warthogs at first glance, but have tiny tusks and no warts. A long mane runs from head to tail. Unlike warthogs, bushpigs are active mainly at night.

These animals are social, living in groups of 8–12: a male, several females, and their young. The dominant boar will keep rival males at bay by erecting its bristly hair, whisking its tail, snapping its jaws and pawing the ground to raise dust. Sparring males push each other around until one retreats.

Bushpig groups spread out when foraging, grunting softly to keep in touch. They dig for roots and bulbs with their tough snouts, but will readily feed on seed pods, earthworms and carrion. When wild fruit is in season, they will butt trees to shake ripe fruit loose. Bushpigs swim well, and wallow in mud to rid themselves of ticks and fleas.

Viewing notes: Nocturnal, and very seldom seen.

A juvenile bushpig.

Eland
Africa's largest antelope

The eland is easily recognised by its massive size, bovine build and tightly spiralling horns. Adult bulls measure up to 1.7m at the shoulder and tip the scales at about 700kg. Despite its bulk, this powerful animal can clear two-metre-high fences.

Eland typically form small herds. Bulls are non-territorial, but become possessive over cows on heat. Rival males lock horns, pushing and twisting until the loser breaks free and runs. As a bull matures, its body becomes greyer, its facial mask darker, and the dewlap under its throat longer. Eland bulls emit a deep clicking sound from their knees as they walk. The purpose of these knee-clicks is not fully understood, but may advertise a bull's size, and therefore its dominant status.

Eland primarily browse, occasionally hooking their horns over high branches to drag the foliage within reach.

Viewing notes: Despite their size, eland are elusive. They are most often seen the north-eastern regions.

Left: Bulls sport a brush of curly hair over the glandular skin on the forehead. It is used to scent-mark the ground. **Above:** Both sexes have horns.

Greater kudu
Crowned with magnificent horns

Kudu bulls sport the longest horns of all Kruger's antelope. These striking spiral horns reach full length – around 130cm – when the bull is about six years old. The animal must tilt its head backwards when running, holding the horns along its spine to keep them from tangling with branches.

Kudus live in small herds. They are highly alert and quick to detect danger, their large ears enabling exceptional hearing. They often step onto anthills to scan their surroundings from a raised vantage point. When alarmed and on the run, kudus curl their tail upwards, revealing a fluffy, white underside. This white 'flag' acts as a beacon to the herd behind it, enabling the group to stick together.

Viewing notes: Best seen in grasslands bordering bushveld, as well as among mopane thickets.

Kudu cows do not have horns. Both sexes have distinctively humped shoulders.

Nyala
An attractively marked species

The nyala falls between the greater kudu and bushbuck in size, males measuring some 115cm at the shoulder. The bull bears lyre-shaped, yellow-tipped horns, and has a slate-grey, handsomely marked coat with shaggy underparts and a mane of hair running down the neck and back. Its yellow-brown lower legs are diagnostic. The ewe is smaller than the bull, chestnut in colour, with no horns.

Nyalas are normally found in small, female-led family groups. Young males are evicted when they are a year old, and join all-male groups until they are old enough to strike out by themselves. Whereas ewes are likely to mix with impala herds, nyala bulls are shy and prefer a solitary existence in thicker bush. Large, temporary groupings may be found around an abundant source of food or water.

Viewing notes: Favours riverine areas with many thickets to hide in. Can usually be seen along the H12 near Skukuza, along the drive from there to Lower Sabie, or along the Levubu River at Pafuri.

The bull (at the back) and ewes differ greatly in appearance.

Bushbuck
Small but fierce

This handsome antelope is yellowish to dark brown, sporting white markings on the flanks, thighs and face. Its markings resemble that of the nyala, but the bushbuck is much smaller, with males measuring about 85cm at the shoulder.

This antelope is non-territorial and solitary, steering clear of other bushbuck if their small home ranges happen to overlap.

A bushbuck typically avoids predators by freezing and lying flat. It is a strong swimmer and may take to water if pursued. Cornered rams fight fiercely, and have been known to gore predators to death with their ridged, twisted horns.

Ewes give birth in dense vegetation. As is usual for antelope, the mother licks the newborn clean and eats the afterbirth so that predators are less likely to smell her young. The calf remains hidden for about four months before venturing out with its mother.

Bushbuck give a bark-like call, which can be heard from kilometres away.

Viewing notes: Always found close to permanent water, preferring dense bush along rivers. The bird hide near Skukuza is a good place to spot them.

Above: Rams raise a crest of hair down their back in display. **Right:** A ewe.

Sable antelope
Beautiful and deadly

Sable bulls are a shiny black, with a sharply contrasting white belly, rump and facial markings. Fittingly, they are known as 'swartwitpens' in Afrikaans, meaning 'black white-stomach'. Cows and young are chestnut brown. Both sexes have an erect mane and long, back-curved horns. Sable have been known to kill lions with these formidable weapons. Bulls use their horns to mark their territory, stripping bark and breaking branches. Rival males frequently clash, and when threat displays escalate to fights, they typically drop to their knees to spar. The dominant bull fathers the young, but the herd is led by an alpha cow.

Viewing notes: Always found within a few kilometres of water, usually in fairly thick bush. Frequently spotted in the north of the Park. Often observed around the Orpen Rocks area and near Phabeni Gate.

Females and young are chestnut brown.

Roan antelope
Large, long-eared antelope

The roan antelope is named for its unmistakable coloration. Its ears can grow up to 30cm long, and sport dark tassels at the tips. It is the Park's second-largest antelope, measuring up to 1.4m at the shoulder.

Roan antelope live in female-led nursery herds, bachelor groups, or as solitary bulls. As with all antelope, a bull will determine whether a cow is on heat by sticking his nose into the stream as she urinates. He then repeatedly and gently taps his foreleg between her hind legs. She will either evade his attention by circling him, or allow mating.

Viewing notes: Fewer than 70 roan antelope are estimated to occur in the Park. Most are found on the north-eastern basalt plains.

Both sexes have scimitar-shaped horns. Calves' horns appear 40 days after birth.

Waterbuck
Robust and shaggy

This large antelope is easily identified by its shaggy grey-brown coat and the white ring around its rump. Males have lyre-shaped, heavily ringed horns. Both sexes have a musky scent that can be smelled a long way downwind.

As the name implies, it is a strong swimmer and is usually found near water. Its coat is near-waterproof, and a waterbuck can wade for hours without water seeping to the skin. It takes to water when danger threatens, where most predators will not follow.

Waterbuck gather in mixed herds, usually with no more than 12 individuals. During dry periods, several herds may converge on available water, merging into a larger, temporary group. Older males typically act as sentries.

Cows usually give birth to a single calf, but twins are occasionally born.

Viewing notes: Only found where there is permanent water.

Above: Mother and young. **Right:** Only the males have horns.

Reedbuck
Athletic antelope with a curious gait

Two reedbuck species occur in the Park. The **common reedbuck** favours lower-lying grasslands, whereas the **mountain reedbuck** grazes on ridges and mountain slopes.

The common reedbuck is the larger of the two, measuring some 95cm at the shoulder. Dark lines run down the front of its forelegs (absent in the mountain reedbuck). Rams of both species have ridged horns that curve forwards, though the horns of the common reedbuck are longer.

Reedbuck live in small family groups. When running, they have a characteristic 'rocking-horse' gait, and curl their tail upwards to display the fluffy white underside. This acts as a beacon for the rest of the family.

As with all antelope, ewes hide their newborn calf, visiting once or twice a day to suckle and clean the young.

Viewing notes: Mountain reedbuck can sometimes be spotted in the Berg-en-Dal area. Common reedbuck are best seen in the grasslands north of Mlondozi and around Shitlhava Dam near Pretoriuskop.

Left: A subadult common reedbuck. **Above:** Mountain reedbuck.

Grey rhebok
Fleet-footed and large-nosed

The grey rhebuck has a thick, woolly coat, long, narrow ears and a large black nose that looks somewhat swollen. The male has short, sharply pointed horns that are nearly straight.

This species runs with a 'rocking-horse' gait and is a good jumper, kicking its fore- and hind legs out stiffly with each leap and flashing its white underparts.

It lives in small family groups of up to 20 animals consisting of the territorial male, its female and their offspring. All four feet possess pedal glands that emit a strong-smelling substance to mark their territory as they walk. When males fight over territory, they snort and stamp their feet. Both sexes hiss and snort at intruders to drive them away.

It typically grazes, but when grass is scarce, it will add flowers, roots, leaves and seeds to its diet.

Viewing notes: Hardly ever seen. Favours mountainous areas and adjacent grasslands in the Malelane section.

The ewe is hornless.

Blue wildebeest
Cattle-like antelope

Wildebeest have a somewhat top-heavy appearance. The head is large and broad, with a black beard and curved horns, and the heavily built, maned shoulders taper to slender hindquarters. Both male and female wildebeest have horns, but those of the male are thicker.

These animals live in herds of up to 30 individuals. They are often seen in the company of other grazers, such as zebras, which feed on longer grasses, thereby creating access to the shorter grasses favoured by wildebeest.

Wildebeest have poor eyesight, but good hearing and an excellent sense of smell. Nomadic by nature, they are known to follow the sound of thunder and the smell of rain to more promising pastures.

Wildebeest calve during the height of summer, when the vegetation is in a fresh flush from summer rains. Newborn calves get to their feet within minutes, and can gallop along with a herd within half an hour.

Viewing notes: Plentiful throughout the Park.

Above: Rival males lock horns. **Right:** Calves are light brown in colour.

Tsessebe
Gawky but speedy

The large, long-faced tsessebe has a distinct purplish gloss to its reddish-brown body. Despite its clumsy-looking appearance, it is the Park's fastest antelope. It can sprint over 70km/h, and can maintain a steady gallop over several kilometres.

Tsessebes are social, and form small herds. Like many antelope, they are seasonal breeders, with all females dropping their calves in the same 30–40-day period. This is an anti-predation strategy. Predators can only catch a limited number of young tsessebes at a time – some calves are bound to survive. Young males are forced out of the herd by the territorial male when they are a year old. They then join bachelor herds until they are around three years, when they start looking for a mate and a territory of their own.

Viewing notes: More common in the north of the Park.

A pregnant cow. Both males and females have horns.

Lichtenstein's hartebeest
Dubious residency

Lichtenstein's hartebeest is yellowish tawny in colour, with a tuft of black hair at the end of its tail. Both sexes have ridged, S-shaped horns and humped shoulders that give the back a sloping appearance.

Herds average about ten individuals, consisting of a territorial bull, several cows and their offspring. Like many territorial antelope, hartebeest mark their home range by ground horning. This is done by dropping to the knees and digging up soil with the horns. They also scent-mark their territory with a tarry substance secreted from glands near its eye. This species has a habit of rubbing its face on its flanks, causing these secretions to leave a dark patch just behind the shoulders.

During the winter rut, the bull may briefly leave its family to acquire more females from other herds. Fights between males are fierce and even fatal. Bulls bellow loudly as they clash.

Viewing notes: A number of these antelope were introduced in the 1980s, but there are few, if any, left in the Park.

This antelope has distinct humped shoulders.

Impala
Common but worth watching

The medium-sized, reddish-brown impala is by far the most abundant large mammal in the Park. These vigilant antelope have keen senses of sight, hearing and smell, and are able to leap up to 12m in a single bound.

Impala herds take three forms: bachelor herds made up of young males; territorial rams with their females; and ewes with young under two years of age.

Breeding is synchronised, with mass birthing occurring at the height of summer (November–December). Since all the young are born at the same time, the odds are that the majority will survive predation attempts. As with all antelope, the mother eats the afterbirth to keep hyaenas and other predators from smelling the vulnerable newborns.

Males use a gland (which looks like a dark brown patch of hair between the horns) as one means of marking territory.

Viewing notes: Very common. Often the first animal visitors see upon starting their safari. The highest concentrations are in the south of the Park.

Above: Mother and calf. **Right:** Only males have horns. The buds start showing a few weeks after birth.

When water is readily available, impala drink daily. They can go weeks without water if necessary, however, as they obtain moisture from their food.

Steenbok
An antelope of cleanly habits

This small antelope is often mistaken for impala, but can be distinguished by its black nose, short tail and solitary habits.

The steenbok (Afrikaans for 'stone buck') is named for the way it stands stock-still when danger approaches, fleeing only at the very last moment. It takes great care in disposing of its droppings: it scrapes a hole in the ground with its front hooves, then deposits the dung in it, and covers it up.

These antelope are mixed feeders. Besides grazing, they dig for roots and bulbs. Since this diet is rich in moisture, they are not dependent on surface water.

They mate for life, and a pair inhabits a common territory.

Viewing notes: Steenbok are found throughout the Park, but occur at higher densities in the open grasslands in the eastern regions.

A subadult male with short horns. Females are hornless.

Klipspringer
The rock hopper

This small, sure-footed antelope inhabits rocky terrain – hence the name klipspringer (Afrikaans for 'rock jumper'). It walks on the very tips of its hooves, the narrow soles and blunt tips enabling precise placement and good traction. The coat has spiny, hollow hairs that insulate this small animal against climatic extremes.

Klipspringers mate for life and are found in pairs or family groups. Rams strike a characteristically motionless pose on top of a high rock while scanning the surroundings. The patch of bare black skin at the corner of this antelope's eye is a gland used to scent-mark its territory. The klipspringer carefully manoeuvres a twig tip into this gland, smearing it with a pungent, sticky substance. Certain ticks exploit this behaviour. They are attracted to the scent, and clamber up the twig to wait for the resident klipspringer's return, then jumping onto their new host.

Viewing notes: Best seen on rocky outcrops.

Above: Only the male has horns. **Right:** A klipspringer scent-marks a twig using the gland at the corner of its eye.

Sharpe's grysbok
A secretive species

This small, solitary antelope is shy by nature, and poorly known as a result. It favours very thick vegetation, and is quick to disappear into it when approached. Its mottled coat blends well with the dappled shade of its habitat.

It eats mainly leaves and young shoots of shrubs and bushes, as well as grass shoots and flowers, but is also partial to the berries of kudu berry and raisin berry trees.

Like several of the Park's antelope species, it has a gland at the corner of its eye, which it uses to scent-mark its territory. Ewes also have a pedal gland on their hind legs, leaving a trail of their highly individual scent as they walk, which allows their young to track their mother through thick bush.

Viewing notes: Rarely spotted. Mainly found in the northern regions in rocky terrain with low bush and grass cover. Generally active at night and occasionally seen in the early mornings and late afternoons.

Females are hornless.

Common (grey) duiker
Shy and solitary

The common duiker, also known as the grey duiker, is distinguished by a black band running from the top of its muzzle to the forehead. It sports a tuft of dark hair on top of its head. Only the male has horns.

It is a solitary species, with males and females only briefly pairing up to mate. There is no set breeding season, and the female bears a single calf. As is usual for antelope, the newborn is quick to get to its feet and is able to sprint from predators on its first day in the world.

The common duiker has acute senses of hearing, eyesight and smell, and is quick to sense danger. When fleeing, it tends to zigzag in an effort to confuse and shake off its pursuer.

Viewing notes: As they prefer thick bush habitats, they can be difficult to spot.

The common duiker can be identified by the black stripe running down its muzzle.

Red duiker
Petite and secretive

The red duiker is smaller than the common duiker, measuring 42cm at the shoulders and weighing no more than 14kg. Its coat has a reddish-orange hue, with some white hairs under the chin and throat, inside the ears and on the tail tip. Both sexes have short horns. The back is rounded, sloping towards the rump.

This species is very secretive, and will bound into thickets at the first sign of an observer. As such, little is known of its habits. It is solitary, but not territorial, and home ranges may overlap. Neighbours use communal dung heaps. It is active at dusk and dawn, foraging on figs and other fruit, as well as leaves and flowers.

Viewing notes: Hardly if ever seen. Favours dense thickets where water is available, thickly wooded ravines and forests.

Rarely seen, the red duiker is a solitary and secretive animal.

Chacma baboon
Sociable troopers

This long-faced baboon is South Africa's largest primate (aside from humans), with males reaching the weight of a small adult human and females smaller, about half the size of a male.

Chacmas are intelligent and gregarious, living in large troops and communicating with grooming, facial expressions and vocalisations. Their strong social network is maintained mostly by grooming and play. Grooming also serves to remove parasites and reduce stress.

They are opportunistic omnivores, feeding on tubers, roots, insects and eggs, sometimes even supplementing their varied diet with freshly killed antelope and the occasional pilfered picnic lunch.

It is easy to determine a baby chacma's age at a glance: clinging under the mother's belly means it is under a month old; riding on her back puts the baby at two to three months old; after three months it moves around independently with the troop.

Viewing notes: Mostly diurnal, chacmas retreat before sunset to the elevated safety of steep hills, high rocks or big trees, to avoid predators.

Above: The canines of a fully grown male are larger than those of a cheetah.
Right: A youngster clings to its mother's back.

Foraging chacma baboons. Troops are mixed, consisting of both males and females. A dominant adult male presides over the group, which has a complex and ever-changing hierarchy. Groups can reach up to 100 members when conditions are good.

Vervet monkey
Pesky resident

Much smaller than chacma baboons, vervet monkeys are grizzled light grey in colour, with black faces and ears contrasted with pale fringing hair and a white forehead stripe.

They live in small, mixed-sex troops of up to 20 individuals, with a clear pecking order. They roost in the relative safety of trees at night, taking cover from predators like leopards, raptors and snakes.

They can become very agitated at the approach of any danger, jumping from tree to tree or hopping about from branch to branch. Many different species are quick to notice vervets' nervousness, and heed the warning signals.

Mostly herbivorous, vervets sometimes eat insects, and eggs and chicks raided from nests, but will eat almost anything they come across, except carrion.

Viewing notes: Practically any road will bring a vervet sighting. They are prevalent in the camping grounds where they go in search of food.

Newborns have pale faces and dark hair. Within 12 weeks of birth their coloration matches that of the adults.

Samango monkey
South Africa's rarest monkey

The shy samango (from the Zulu name 'iNsimango') is seldom over 9kg in weight, with females being half the size of the males. These monkeys may be mistaken for the commonplace vervets but fluffy cheek tufts, a patch of hair above the eyes and a darker coat help to tell them apart.

Moving around the relative safety of the canopy, samangos feed mostly on fruit, leaves, flowers and insects, filling their cheek pouches, hamster-like, with food to consume later.

Highly social, these monkeys live in troops of around 20 individuals, with a single adult male leading a harem of females and young. Only the male calls loudly, giving a low, carrying boom, which guides the troop in its sometimes acrobatic movements around the trees, and also producing staccato 'pyow' sounds. Females occasionally make softer chirps and clicks.

Like the chacmas and vervets, samangos pamper and groom other members of the troop, reinforcing social connections.

Viewing notes: Occurs in forests in the northern parts.

Long cheek tufts and a thicker, darker coat distinguish samangos from vervets.

Greater bushbaby
Large, bushy-tailed primate

The greater bushbaby can measure up to 75cm from nose to tail tip. Over half its length is made up of its long, fluffy tail, however, and adult males weigh no more than 1.25kg (females are a bit lighter). They have unmistakeably large eyes and ears.

Bushbabies emerge at dusk to forage, feeding mainly on fruit and tree gum and occasionally snacking on insects, birds and reptiles. They live in stable family groups of two to six animals. They have up to 12 resting places within their home range and never sleep in one site for a long stretch of time.

The sharp teeth are used mainly in grooming. To scent-mark its territory, a bushbaby urinates on its hands and feet and leaves damp, smelly prints as it travels.

Viewing notes: Mainly seen on night drives where the lights reflect in their eyes as they jump from tree to tree.

Bushbabies are thickly furred.

Lesser bushbaby
Tiny, bug-eyed acrobat

The lesser bushbaby is much smaller than the greater bushbaby. Tipping the scales at 150g, this tiny primate is barely a tenth of its larger relative's weight. It is incredibly agile, leaping between branches up to three metres apart – in the dark, no less. To make the most of the available light, its bulging eyes are very large – so large that they cannot move in their sockets. To survey its surroundings, a bushbaby can swivel its head a full 180 degrees.

Bushbabies feed on insects and tree sap. They forage alone, but sleep in groups. When venturing to the ground, they hop on their back legs, the forearms making no contact with the ground.

Females have two litters per year, typically twins or triplets. Young can crawl an hour after being born. At two weeks old, their teeth erupt and they begin catching their own food.

Viewing notes: Bushbabies emerge after sunset, and are most active before midnight. They are often seen in trees around camps and on night drives.

Bushbabies have opposable thumbs and big toes. Their palms and digits are padded for good grip.

Tree squirrel
Agile tree dweller

This small brown squirrel is about 35cm long, half of which is its fluffy tail. Its conspicuous black whiskers are about 5cm in length.

It lives in small family groups of two to eight individuals. The group forages together, feeding on flowers, leaves, berries and grass. Family members frequently groom each other, enabling them to quickly recognise one another by their scent.

Tree squirrels have sharp hearing and eyesight, and are quick to spot a threat. When a predator such as a snake or bird approaches, the squirrels may gang up against it, flicking their tails and making loud clicking sounds to intimidate the intruder. This is known as mobbing.

They are very agile and can jump up to two metres from branch to branch. Holes in trees are used as nesting and breeding sites.

Viewing notes: Active by day. Common wherever there are trees.

When mature, males weigh a mere 200g.

Springhare
'Kangaroo' of the Kruger

Though called a hare and built like a dwarf kangaroo, this species is a type of rodent. It hops on long, powerful legs and can bound two metres at a time when chased. Its long tail acts as a rudder when fleeing at speed. If caught, the springhare will tear at the predator with the sharp claws on its large hindlimbs. Its forelegs are smaller, and used for digging and clasping its food – mainly grasses and roots.

Springhares are skilled diggers. They excavate personal burrows, which can be dozens of metres long, and use their broad incisor teeth to gnaw through roots blocking the way. They sleep standing, with the head tucked between the hind legs.

Viewing notes: This nocturnal rodent is best seen on night drives. Its large eyes reflect bright white circles in torchlight, bobbing as it hops along.

The springhare has a long, bushy, black-tipped tail.

Porcupine
An unmistakable rodent

This spiky rodent is large, weighing up to 19kg. Sharp, black-and-white quills cover the upperparts of its body, and can be up to 50cm in length.

When danger threatens, a porcupine erects its quills, so as to appear double in size. It stamps its feet, grunts, and noisily rattles the long, hollow spines on its tail. This is an attempt to intimidate predators who wish to knock the porcupine over and get to its soft, unprotected underparts. Quills cannot be 'shot' at attackers. Instead, the animal will run backwards or sideways into its attacker. Quills are easily detached from the porcupine, and remain embedded in the attacker's flesh, typically the mouth and paws. These wounds may become septic, which can prove fatal.

Young are born with soft spines, which harden in the air.

Viewing notes: Nocturnal and very rarely spotted. Occasionally seen on night drives on the H10.

The porcupine is Africa's largest rodent.

Elephant shrews
Long-snouted rodents

Elephant shrews are neither true shrews nor related to elephants. They are named for their long, almost trunk-like snouts. Fully grown, these small rodents weigh only 40–60g. Their coloration differs depending on their habitat, and can be reddish yellow, yellowish brown, grey, or anything in between. Three species have been recorded in the Park.

They are active during the day, especially in the early morning when they come out to feed on insects, such as ants and grasshoppers. They are also known to feed on seeds and fruit.

Elephant shrews are highly territorial. They dig their own burrows, but sometimes take over other rodents' nests. Pairs mate for life, and females produce about five litters of two young each year.

Birds of prey, snakes and wild cats are their biggest enemies.

The elongated snout is characteristic.

Mice
Tiny and short-lived

Although several species of mouse occur in the Park, the typical visitor will be lucky to catch even a glimpse of these small, shy rodents.

Mice typically live in groups, excavating chambered burrows and building nests made up of dry vegetation inside. To dig, a mouse loosens the soil with its incisor teeth, picks up a load of debris in its mouth, and deposits it outside the entrance. Some species build their nests in the holes of trees, whereas others may nest in rock crevices or beneath rotting tree trunks.

Mice mostly feed at night. Diets vary among species, and can include plant parts (especially seeds), fruit and small invertebrates.

A typical mouse lives only about five months, owing to predation by reptiles, mammals and birds, especially owls.

Mice live in chambered burrows.

Rats
Prolific breeders

Wild rats may have a reputation as dirty pests, but they are in truth fastidious self-groomers, and crucial to the food chain. Many different mammals, reptiles and birds rely on them as a source of food. Rats are larger than mice, and tend to live longer – about two to five years.

Most rat species are nocturnal, but some feed during the day. Their long, sensitive whiskers help them detect obstacles while navigating in the dark. Although they are good climbers, most prefer being on the ground when foraging for food. Omnivorous, they eat prey such as insects and invertebrates in addition to grasses and seeds. Most rats can swim and will forage in aquatic environments.

A female produces several litters each year. She has six pairs of nipples, and can birth and raise up to 12 young at a time.

Left: Agoni vlei rat. **Above:** The well-known invasive black rat occurs in the Park.

Common molerat
Aggressive burrow dweller

Molerats live in underground colonies. They have short, silky fur and vary in colour, yellow albinos being especially common. Their eyesight and sense of smell are very poor, but they are extremely sensitive to vibrations. Long bristle-like hairs on the feet pick up the slightest movements in and on the ground surrounding them.

Molerats inhabit a variety of soils – from sandy to rocky. The main burrow is 15–20cm under the surface, with several side tunnels and nesting chambers at a deeper level. They are very active after rains, extending their burrows while the ground is soft. To get rid of excavated soil, they throw up molehills along the main burrow.

They feed on fleshy roots, bulbs, tubers and succulent underground rhizomes.

When faced with danger, they are aggressive: they grunt and squeak, then throw the head back, opening the mouth to display formidable incisor teeth.

Molerats have large incisor teeth.

Hedgehog
Prickly customer

With its pointed face and short, sharp spines covering the flanks and back, the hedgehog is unmistakeable. It rolls into a ball to protect its soft belly when confronted with a predator.

It is a solitary animal with no permanent home, simply curling up under matted grass, debris and shaded bushes or in holes when it is time to rest. It is active at night.

It is an omnivore and the largest part of its diet consists of insects, termites and moths. It will also eat vegetable matter, small mice, frogs, lizards and small chicks and eggs of birds.

During summer, it builds up a thick layer of fat under the skin. As colder weather approaches, it becomes lethargic and loses its appetite, entering a hibernation period that may last six weeks. In this time, it lives off its stored fat, much as bears do.

The sharp-snouted face is dark.

Aardvark (antbear)
An unforgettable sight

This unusual animal has a long, pig-like snout, rabbit-like ears, a humped back and powerful, clawed feet. The name 'aardvark' means 'earth pig' in Afrikaans. Fittingly, it is a skilled digger, excavating burrows with multiple chambers. It is quick to abandon old burrows and dig new ones, and many other species use or modify abandoned aardvark burrows as underground dens.

It is active at night, travelling long distances to find its prey: termites. It rapidly rips the mound open with its strong claws, pushes its snout inside, and licks up the inhabitants, their larvae and eggs with its long, sticky tongue. It eats ants when termites are scarce, especially during the dry season.

Aardvarks are solitary, meeting only to mate.

Viewing notes: More common in the northern half of the Park, where there is an abundance of termites and termite hills. Also spotted on the road from Skukuza to Lower Sabie.

Aardvarks are avid diggers.

Pangolin
Armoured anteater

The pangolin is unique – it is Africa's only scale-clad mammal. Sturdy, brown, overlapping scales cover its head, back and tail, and make up a third of its weight. The scales are composed of keratin, the same substance our fingernails are made of. When threatened, the pangolin curls up into an armoured ball, near-impenetrable to the claws and fangs of even large predators. Its sharp-edged tail also makes a formidable slicing weapon.

A pangolin can grow up to a metre from nose to tail. Remarkably, its tongue is longer than its body when fully unfolded and extended. The tongue is sticky, and is used to collect ants and occasionally termites.

Viewing notes: Nocturnal and secretive. Most prevalent where there is an abundance of ant and termite hills, especially in the northern half of the Park. It has also been spotted on the road from Skukuza to Lower Sabie.

A pangolin curls into a ball, tucking its head under the armoured tail.

Rock hyrax
Social and sun-loving

These small, sturdy mammals are highly sociable, living in colonies of up to 30 individuals. They are found in and among rocks, piles of loose boulders and rocky outcrops which provide them with shelter and a place to hide from predators, such as eagles, leopards and caracals. The soles of their feet are thickly padded and have glands that keep the feet moist. This gives them extra traction when jumping from rock to rock. Hyraxes are known to bark in alarm, and have over 20 different calls.

Hyraxes eat a variety of plants, grasses and wild figs and are able to go for many days without water owing to the moisture they obtain from their food. They are immune to the toxins of several poisonous shrubs.

Viewing notes: Inhabits rocky outcrops. Often seen basking in the sun.

They are variable in colour, from yellow-buff to reddish or greyish brown.

Scrub hare
Fluffy and fast

A large hare, measuring some 60cm from nose to tail tip. Females are larger and heavier than males.

The scrub hare is solitary and nocturnal, lying up under bushes during the day. It folds its ears back to conceal itself better, and relies on camouflage when approached – only speeding off at the last moment. When fleeing, it zigzags to confuse pursuers. Typically silent, it will squeal loudly, kick savagely with its back feet, and bite if seized by a predator.

In the winter, it feeds on green grass. When this becomes scarce, it will also feed on the stems and rhizomes of dried grass, as well as on leaves of other plants.

Viewing notes: Nocturnal. Seen on night drives, where it tends to run in front of the vehicle, staying in the headlights while zigzagging.

The hind legs are much longer than the front legs.

Bats
Unique flying mammals

Bats are the only mammals capable of flight. Their forelimbs are modified into webbed wings. The finger bones are greatly elongated, with thin membranes of skin stretched between them. Since each finger can be moved independently, bats are capable of impressive aerial acrobatics – hovering, swooping and turning in the darkness.

Over 40 species of bat occur in the Park. Some hunt insects, others feed on fruit, or nectar and pollen. They play a crucial role in the ecosystem by keeping insect populations in check, and by spreading seeds and pollen, helping plants to reproduce.

Bats are active at night. To navigate in the dark, a bat emits high-pitched calls. The sound bounces off nearby objects, such as trees, or the bat's prey. By listening for the echo, the bat is able to perceive its surroundings, a technique known as echolocation.

Left: Mauritian tomb bat. **Above:** Peters's epauletted fruit bats.

Insect-eating bats can detect the tiniest of prey, and catch flying insects at a rate of up to two per second.

Bats typically have set breeding seasons. The young are hairless or lightly furred, with long hind legs to hold onto their mothers when roosting. In several species, the female carries her young while foraging.

Viewing notes: During the day, many Peters's epauletted fruit bats roost under the eaves of the shops at Skukuza and under the umbrellas at the food court there. Large colonies – up to hundreds of individuals – hang from the branches of evergreen trees in camps such as the one outside Satara's reception area. Mauritian tomb bats roost in smaller colonies (typically about five, but occasionally as many as 30 individuals), hanging from the branches of large trees or under the eaves of buildings. These bats can be recognised by their watchful behaviour when at roost. They give the impression of always being awake.

Above: Mauritian tomb bat. **Right:** A female Peters's epauletted fruit bat and her young.

172

Glossary

Aquatic: Living in water

Arboreal: Living in trees

Browse: To feed on high-growing vegetation, such as leaves

Canine teeth: Sharp teeth behind the incisors, enlarged in carnivores and used to stab

Carnivore: An animal that feeds on other animals

Carrion: Decaying flesh

Diurnal: Active during the day

Dorsal: On the back

Forage: Search for food

Gestation: Pregnancy, the period between conception and birth

Graze: To feed on grass

Gregarious: Living together in colonies or groups

Habitat: The natural home of a particular species

Herbivore: An animal that feeds on plants

Incisors: Cutting teeth at the front of the mouth

Invertebrates: Creatures that lack a backbone, such as insects, worms and spiders

Midden: Dung heap

Molars: Grinding teeth at the back of the mouth

Nocturnal: Active at night

Omnivore: An animal that feeds on both plants and animals

Pre-orbital: Situated in front of the eye socket

Prehensile: Capable of clasping

Raptors: Birds of prey

Regurgitate: Vomit

Rut: A period when the urge to breed is displayed

Scavenger: An animal that feeds on other animals' kills

Solitary: Living alone

Terrestrial: Living on the ground

Territorial: Defending an area

Weaning: Transitioning from mother's milk to other food

Whelping: Giving birth

Picture credits

Index